DECORATIVE SILHOUETTES OF THE TWENTIES

FOR DESIGNERS & CRAFTSMEN

SELECTED AND INTRODUCED BY
Jo Anne C. Day

DOVER PUBLICATIONS, INC., NEW YORK

Published in Canada by General Publishing Company, Ltd., 30 Lesmill Road, Don Mills, Toronto,
Ontario.
Published in the United Kingdom by Constable
and Company, Ltd.

*Decorative Silhouettes of the Twenties for De-
signers and Craftsmen* is a new work first published
by Dover Publications, Inc., in 1975.

DOVER *Pictorial Archive* SERIES

This book belongs to the Dover Pictorial Archive
Series. You may use the designs and illustrations for
graphics and crafts applications, free and without spe-
cial permission, provided that you include no more than
ten in the same publication or project. (For permission
for additional use, please write to Dover Publications,
Inc., 31 East 2nd Street, Mineola, N.Y. 11501.)
However, republication or reproduction in any illus-
tration by any other graphic service whether it be in a
book or in any other design resource is strictly pro-
hibited.

International Standard Book Number: 0-486-23152-6
Library of Congress Catalog Card Number: 73-89255

Manufactured in the United States of America
Dover Publications, Inc.
31 East 2nd Street
Mineola, N.Y. 11501

INTRODUCTION

The 84 silhouettes in this book are reproduced from a rare collection of German die-cuts manufactured in the 1920s. To the best of my knowledge, such items are no longer produced, and it was good fortune to come across so many of such high quality. Ever since the rage for silhouettes in the eighteenth century, this art form has been especially cherished and cultivated in Germany, and the present group reflects this honored tradition most creditably.

The subjects, though, are universal: fashionable ladies, pairs of lovers, Pierrots and Columbines, butterflies, shepherdesses, musicians, picnics, boating parties, galleons, coaches, Japanese scenes. The contemporary dress is that of the Twenties, and even where the costumes are reminiscent of the eighteenth or nineteenth century, the characteristic gestures and the whole mood are of the Twenties, too. Many of the subjects come in pairs, which are kept together in the book.

The original die-cuts were sold for decorative purposes. They were often mounted and framed, or even transferred directly to a plain painted wall. As reproduced here, they can be enjoyed for their artistic value and framed as pictures, but their applicability does not end there! Surfaces of wood, tin, paper or plaster will accept the transfer of a silhouette if they are free of grease and dirt. Enthusiasts of the art of decoupage will find that these designs adapt themselves beautifully to the many and various projects of this craft. Original greeting cards (particularly valentines) can also be created with these designs. The open, lace-like designs of these silhouettes make them perfect for transferring to smooth, light-colored lampshades. The gleam of light penetrating through the shade illuminates the silhouette in a most attractive way. For this purpose, the silhouette should be made translucent and impervious to moisture, as follows:

Each page or silhouette is cut fully from this book. A mixture of 50% *boiled* linseed oil and 50% turpentine is applied with a rag to both sides of the silhouette until it is thoroughly saturated. The oil-treated silhouette is then placed on a dry, clean surface or hung to dry. The rag is immersed in water and destroyed immediately. Spontaneous combustion can occur if the rag is stored for later use. The silhouette will dry to the touch in about ten minutes. When dry, any trimming of the silhouette can be done with scissors or a mat knife.

Transferring the trimmed silhouette requires two steps. First, take the silhouette and center it on the object that is to be decorated. Make the fewest and tiniest chalk marks possible to serve as a guide to the final placement of the silhouette. These marks can be later brushed off or erased. Secondly, glue must be applied to the *back* of the silhouette. Use a spray adhesive. Any good art-supply store will stock spray rubber cement for mounting photographs. Conventional glues will warp the paper and will cause the silhouette to dry wrinkled on a smooth surface. Place the silhouette face down on a clean sheet of newspaper and spray lightly with the adhesive. Allow the adhesive to become tacky (this takes about 30 seconds) before carefully picking up the silhouette, flipping it and pressing it to the waiting surface. Smooth the silhouette from the center to the outer edges so no air pockets can form underneath. Practice this technique several times without the adhesive since there will be no second chance. Use a clean sheet of newspaper for each spraying, so that the adhesive residue on the previous sheet will not be transferred to the front of the next silhouette. Varnishing the finished project is not necessary unless desired.

PLATE 1

PLATE 2

PLATE 3

PLATE 4

PLATE 5

PLATE 6

PLATE 7

PLATE 8

PLATE 9

PLATE 10

PLATE 11

PLATE 12

PLATE 13

PLATE 14

PLATE 15

PLATE 16

PLATE 17

PLATE 18

PLATE 19

PLATE 20

PLATE 21

PLATE 22

PLATE 23

PLATE 24

PLATE 25

PLATE 26

PLATE 27

PLATE 28

PLATE 29

PLATE 30

PLATE 31

PLATE 32

PLATE 33

PLATE 34

PLATE 35

PLATE 36

PLATE 37

PLATE 38

PLATE 39

PLATE 40

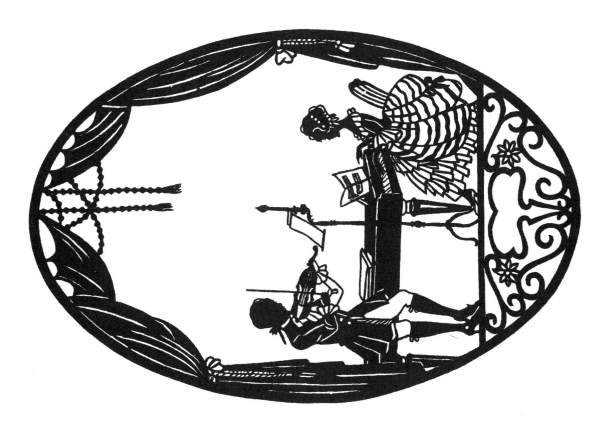

PLATE 41

PLATE 42

PLATE 43

PLATE 44

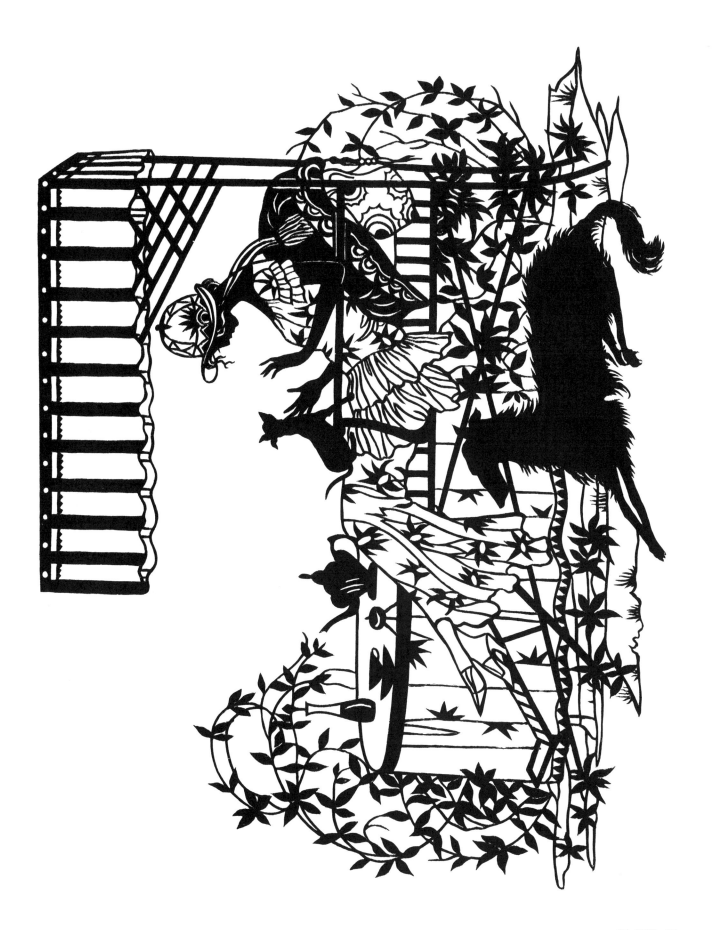

PLATE 45

PLATE 46

PLATE 47

PLATE 48

PLATE 49

PLATE 50

PLATE 51

PLATE 52

PLATE 53

PLATE 54

PLATE 55

PLATE 56

PLATE 57

PLATE 58

PLATE 59

PLATE 60

PLATE 61

PLATE 62

PLATE 63

PLATE 64

PLATE 65

PLATE 66

PLATE 67

PLATE 68

PLATE 69

PLATE 70

PLATE 71

PLATE 72

PLATE 73

PLATE 74

PLATE 75

PLATE 76